Animales del zoológico / Zoo Animals

LAS NUTRIAS
OTTERS
AT THE ZOO

Seth Lynch

Traducido por / Translated by Esther Ortiz

Gareth Stevens
PUBLISHING

Please visit our website, www.garethstevens.com. For a free color catalog of all our high-quality books, call toll free 1-800-542-2595 or fax 1-877-542-2596.

Library of Congress Cataloging-in-Publication Data

Names: Lynch, Seth, author.
Title: Las nutrias / Otters at the zoo / Seth Lynch.
Description: New York : Gareth Stevens Publishing, [2020] | Series: Animales del zoológico / Zoo animals | Includes index.
Identifiers: LCCN 2018039580| ISBN 9781538243619 (library bound)
Subjects: LCSH: Otters–Juvenile literature. | Zoo animals–Juvenile literature.
Classification: LCC QL737.C25 L95 2020 | DDC 599.769–dc23
LC record available at https://lccn.loc.gov/2018039580

First Edition

Published in 2020 by
Gareth Stevens Publishing
111 East 14th Street, Suite 349
New York, NY 10003

Translator: Esther Ortiz
Editor, English: Therese Shea
Designer: Katelyn E. Reynolds

Photo credits: Cover, p. 1 John And Penny/Shutterstock.com; p. 5 Anna Moskvina/Shutterstock.com; p. 7 (top left) Max Allen/Shutterstock.com; p. 7 (top right) Curioso/Shutterstock.com; p. 7 (bottom left) ostill/Shutterstock.com; p. 7 (bottom right) rbrown10/Shutterstock.com; p. 9 Maurice Volmeyer/Shutterstock.com; p. 11 Keneva Photography/Shutterstock.com; p. 13 Jennifer Krafsky/Shutterstock.com; pp. 15, 24 (tail) buteo/Shutterstock.com; pp. 17, 24 (webbed) guentermanaus/Shutterstock.com; p. 19 allixout/Shutterstock.com; p. 21 Kjersti Joergensen/Shutterstock.com; p. 23 © iStockphoto.com/shank_ali.

Printed in the United States of America

CPSIA compliance information: Batch #CS19GS: For further information contact Gareth Stevens, New York, New York at 1-800-542-2595.

Contenido

Contents

Veo nutrias
en el zoológico.
¡Aprendo mucho!

I see otters
at the zoo.
I learn a lot!

Hay 13 tipos
de nutrias.

There are 13 kinds
of otters.

La mayoría vive
cerca de los ríos.

Most otters live
near rivers.

La nutria marina
vive en el océano.

The sea otter lives
in the ocean.

Las nutrias nadan bien.

Otters swim well.

Tienen una cola plana.

They have a flat tail.

Tienen patas palmeadas.

They have webbed feet.

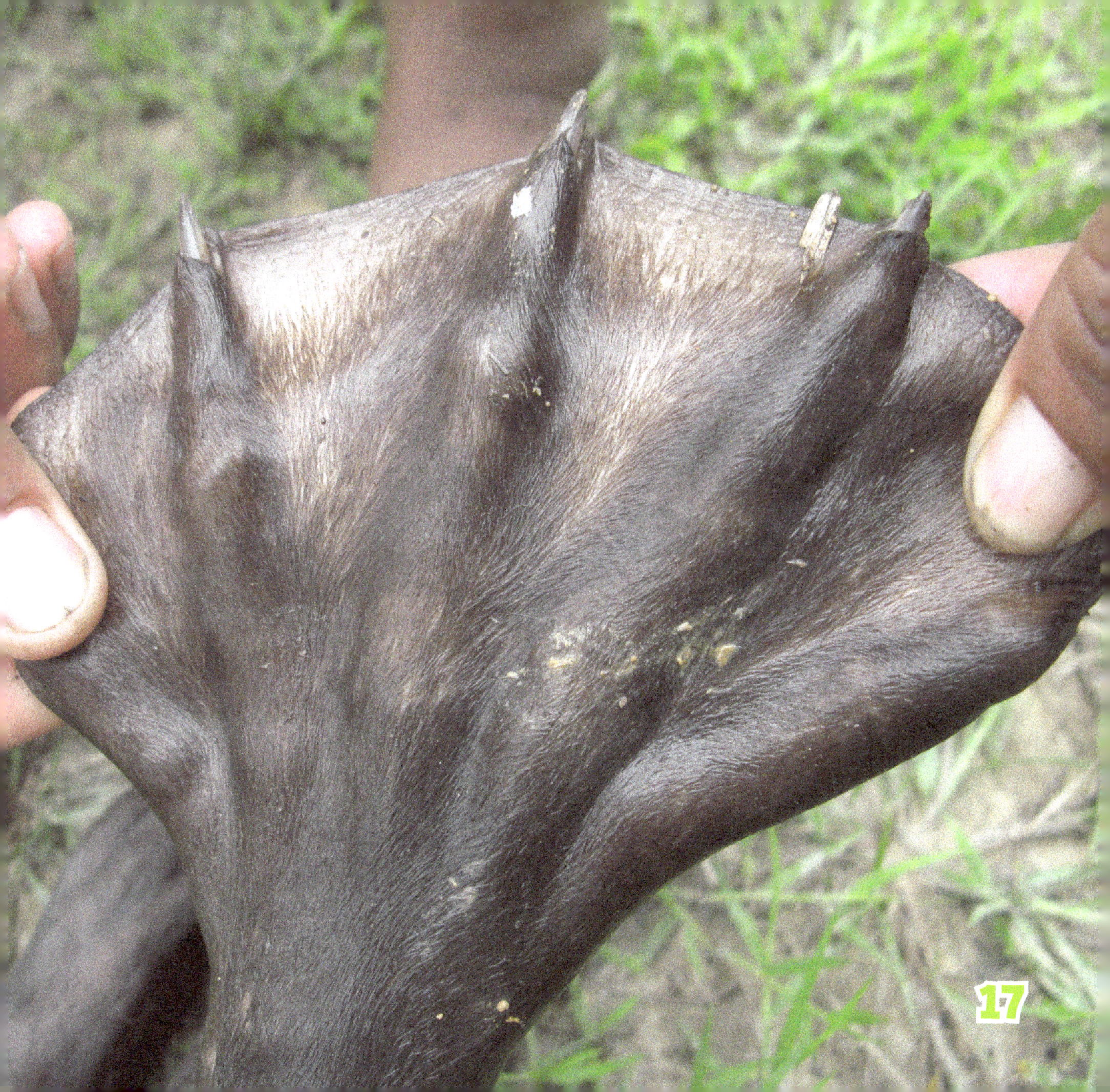

Tienen pelaje grueso.
Las mantiene abrigadas.

They have thick fur.
It keeps them warm.

Las nutrias
comen pescado.
También comen
otros animales de agua.

....

Otters eat fish.
They eat other
water animals, too.

¡Les encanta jugar!
Me gustan las nutrias
del zoológico.

....

Otters love to play!
I like the otters
at the zoo!

Palabras que debes aprender
Words to Know

(la) cola
tail

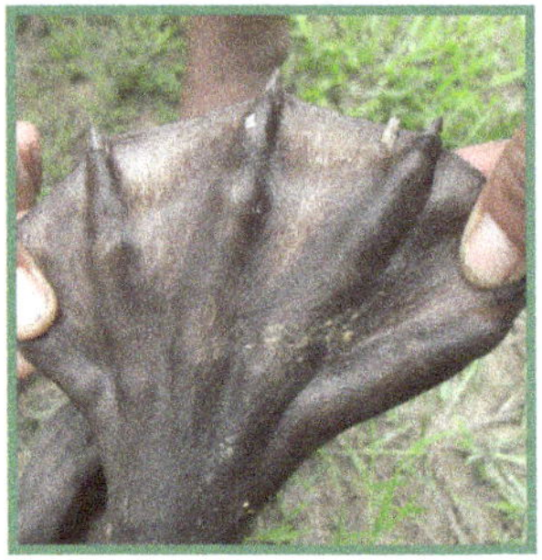

palmeada
webbed

Índice/Index